This Bing book belongs to:

....

Copyright © 2024 Acamar Films Ltd

The *Bing* television series is created by Acamar Films and Brown Bag Films
and adapted from the original books by Ted Dewan.

Ice Cream Surprise is based on the original story 'Ice Cream' written by Ted Dewan, Lucy Murphy, Mikael Shields and An Vrombaut.
It was adapted from the original story by Lauren Holowaty for HarperCollins *Children's Books*.

HarperCollins *Children's Books* is a division of HarperCollins*Publishers* Ltd
1 London Bridge Street, London SE1 9GF

www.harpercollins.co.uk

HarperCollins*Publishers*
Macken House, 39/40 Mayor Street Upper, Dublin 1, D01 C9W8

1 3 5 7 9 10 8 6 4 2

ISBN: 978-0-00-861953-4

Printed in Malaysia

ICE CREAM SURPRISE

HarperCollins *Children's Books*

Round the corner, not far away,
Bing is on his way to the park today!

Just then, Bing hears something.
It's the familiar chimes of Gilly's ice-cream van . . .

Pling, pling! Plingy-pling-pling!

"Flop!" gasps Bing. "It's Gilly!
Can we have an ice cream, Flop? *Please?*"

"Why not," says Flop. "Now, I wonder where Gilly is?"

"Oh, there she is!" says Bing, pointing.

Gilly's ice-cream van is going into the park. Bing waves but she doesn't see him.

"Hurry, Flop!" says Bing, racing to the corner.

"Oh no! Red bunny," says Bing when they
see the red traffic lights at the crossing.

"Green bunny will be back soon," says Flop.
"Now, what flavour ice cream would you like?"

"Hmm. Yummy carrot," decides Bing.

The lights change to the green bunny
and Bing and Flop cross the road.

"Let's . . . go, go, go, go, go, go!"

But when they enter the park, Gilly is nowhere to be seen!

"Hmm, where is she?" asks Bing.

"Let's have a listen," suggests Flop.

"Quick!" says Bing,
leading Flop over the bridge
towards the ice-cream van.

"Okay," says Flop, following.

Bing starts to run. "Come on!" he says.
"Let's get some ice cream!"

Just as they spot Gilly on the other side of the pond,
Bing sees the bridge is blocked.

"Oh no!" he cries.

"Sorry," says the park worker. "We're giving this bridge
a lick of paint, so you'll have to go round the other way."

"Oh, but we're getting our ice cream," says Bing.
"And Gilly's right there. And NOW she's going!"

"Ah, I see. Oh, go on then," says the park worker kindly.
"You can sneak through."

"Thank you!" cheers Bing. But just as they
get through, Gilly drives off again.

"Ohh!" sighs Bing.

"Don't worry, Bing. It's no big thing," says Flop.
"We can catch her."

"Okay," says Bing. "Come on, Flop!"

Pling, pling! Plingy-pling-pling!

Gilly stops for some customers.

"Gilly!" calls Bing, waving. "Wait for me!"

Gilly serves her customers and is about to drive off,
when Popsie sees Bing . . .

Woof! Woof! Woof!

"What's all this fuss then, Popsie?" asks Gilly.
She spots Bing and Flop. "Oh, I see! Our last two customers."

"Hello, Gilly! Hello, Popsie! We ran and ran
after you," says Bing, panting.

"Then you must be *very* hot," says Gilly.
"What would you like to cool down?"

"Oh, can I have a carrot ice cream with chocolate sauce in a cone with ears, please?" asks Bing.

"Here you go," says Gilly.

"Thank you," says Bing. "Oh, yum!"

"I'll have one of your fruit kebabs with chocolate
sauce, please, Gilly," says Flop.

Gilly **squirts** the chocolate sauce on the fruit. "Here you go."

"Oh, lovely," says Flop. "Thank you, Gilly."

"You're welcome," says Gilly.

"See you soon," she calls, waving to Flop
and Bing as she drives off.

"Thanks, Gilly," says Flop. "Byesie-bye."

Woof! Woof! Woof!

"Bye-bye, Popsie!" says Bing, waving his arms
in the air and jumping up and down excitedly . . .

Suddenly, Bing's ice cream falls out
of the cone and on to the ground.

SPLAT!

"Oh no!" cries Bing. "My *ice cream!*"

Bing stares at his ice cream.
"Oh no! Can you put it back, Flop?" he asks.

"I can't, Bing," says Flop.
"It's all dirty now. I'm sorry."

"**Ohhh**, now Gilly's gone," says Bing.
"And I really *did* want my ice cream.
It was so yummy-delicious and now it's mucky."

Flop scoops up the ice cream with a tissue. "Come on,"
he says to Bing, walking over to the rubbish bin.

"Here, could you hold this for me, please,
Bing?" says Flop, passing Bing his fruit kebab.

Bing takes it and sits down on the bandstand steps,
while Flop puts the mucky ice cream in the bin.

"It's all **drippy**, Flop," says Bing, holding up Flop's kebab as the chocolate sauce drips down.

"Ooh, well, you'd better give it a lick then," says Flop.

LICK! LICK! LICK!

"I haven't got an ice cream, Flop," says Bing sadly.
"And Gilly's gone and I've got *nothing.*"

"Well, you still have your cone . . . **and** it looks
like you've got a fruit kebab!" Flop chuckles.

"That's *yours,* Flop," says Bing.

"Would you like to share it with me, Bing?" asks Flop.

"What's your favourite bit?" asks Flop.

"Err . . . I do like banana," says Bing.
Flop tips some banana into Bing's cone.

"Ooh, how about some melon?" says Flop, popping that in too.

"Yummy-delicious! Thank you, Flop," says Bing.

Bing looks at Flop's fruit kebab. "I do like pineapple too."

"Here, of course," says Flop. "Now it's a lovely *fruit* cone."

"Yummy-delicious!" says Bing.

"Indeed. Yummy-delicious!" agrees Flop.

**Dropping your ice cream . . .
it's a Bing thing!**